ONEIROMANCE
(an epithalamion)

Kathleen Rooney

Winner of the 2007 Gatewood Prize
Selected by Patty Seyburn

CHICAGO

ALSO BY KATHLEEN ROONEY

Poetry Collection
That Tiny Insane Voluptuousness, with Elisa Gabbert
(Otoliths, 2008)

Poetry Chapbooks
Something Really Wonderful, with Elisa Gabbert
(dancing girl press, 2007)

Local Girl Makes Good
(NewSouth Books, 2002)

Nonfiction
Reading with Oprah: The Book Club That Changed America
(University of Arkansas Press, 2005; 2nd edition 2008)

ISBN-13: 978-0-9786172-3-3
ISBN-10: 0-9786172-3-1

LIBRARY OF CONGRESS CONTROL NUMBER: 2008930073

Book design: Cathy Nieciecki
Cover art: Carrie Scanga, 2008

Switchback Books
Brandi Homan, *Editor-in-Chief*
Hanna Andrews and Becca Klaver, *Founding Editors*
Addie Palin and Melissa Severin, *Contest Editors*
PO Box 478868
Chicago, IL 60647
editors@switchbackbooks.com
www.switchbackbooks.com

A dream can be an escape. A dream can be a place of refuge, a place of denial, a place of exploration. The dream as topos in *Oneiromance (an epithalamion)* is all of these locations and more. The dreams take place in specific locations, among them: Brazil and Illinois. Among them: in the sidereal float, the empyreal imagination. The dreams can be based in wish fulfillment, in anxiety, in the exotic and mundane lanes of the imagination. Kathleen Rooney assumes all of these possibilities, as well as the roles of bride and groom. She does not reserve the questions and doubts for her female persona, but ladens her grooms with equal fear of abandonment, self-annihilation, or at least, abnegation. As well as the quality of wonder.

The subject of said dreams is, obviously, marriage, and its sidecar issues: commitment, tradition, responsibility, fidelity, complacency. By engaging these issues in the subconscious venue, the theatricality of marriage takes precedence. Like biblical Joseph or perhaps the Witch of Endor, Rooney is a diviner of dream, as promised in the book's title. That said title contains the word "romance" conjures up all sorts of flying monkeys: will marriage be a dream, idyllic? Or is the idea of a successful marriage so unrealistic that it can only be promulgated within a dream and lived in a dream-state? Is the notion of cohesion between two people more the collusion of a besotted collective consciousness? This collection of poems deftly explores these questions, employing an often formal impulse to give the potential chaos of dream a willingly illusory sense of order.

Much of this work has an ekphrastic quality, as though Rooney fashioned the scene and then described and interpreted it, amending its components as she goes, the landscape fluid as human nature. The Brazilian Wedding Dream poems feel like Chagall's paintings of floating lovers (such as *The Bridal Pair at the Eiffel Tower*, 1938) rendered in language. For her visual component, Rooney turns to her sister, a photographer, present in many of the poems: they are a pair of brides. The two sisters form a different coupling, one that is both threatened and enhanced by the pending nuptials, but they are united in their lack of mooring in the face of the matrimonial leap.

In every epithalamion, the discussion of love coexists with references to death, and risk is vital to the enterprise for this author—one of the appeals of marriage is its degree of difficulty, and its flirtation with the idea of eternity. "*May you love always. May you not die alone*" ("Brazilian Wedding: Dream no. 6"), she writes, and quotes Sir Thomas Aquinas in no. 7: "If the highest aim of a captain / were to preserve his ship, he would keep / it in port forever." In the collection's final section, the Niagara Falls Scrapbook poems bring risk to the forefront of consciousness; one poem details the fifteen people who have "gone over / in a device." These poems detail both the various devices and artifice involved in the emotional and intellectual preparation for and aftermath of the wedding, as well as the inherent symbology of ceremony and ritual. The event serves not only as a turning point for Rooney, but as its own version of a poetic crossing, from singularity to unity, from a lone voice to hearing voices, which Rooney adroitly channels, translates, performs.

In Coleridge's notebooks, he wrote: "If a man could pass thro' Paradise in a Dream, & have a flower presented to him as a pledge that his Soul had really been there, & found that flower in his hand when he awoke—Aye? and what then?" *Oneiromance (an epithalamion)* considers whether the ethereal nature of paradise can coexist with the pragmatics of daily life—how likely is it that two souls can unite? Is this even desirable? "If ever two were one, then surely we," wrote Anne Bradstreet. Kathleen Rooney questions whether such certainty is possible and desirable, whether desire is possible in the face of certainty. While the mind—smart, provocative—frets, debates, these poems weave responses around the unerring call (but what is the location?) of the heart.

—Patty Seyburn
Judge of the 2007 Gatewood Prize

TABLE OF CONTENTS

Prologue: Oneiromance   1

I.
Brazilian Wedding: Dream no. 1   5
Brazilian Wedding: Dream no. 2   7
Brazilian Wedding: Dream no. 3   8
Brazilian Wedding: Dream no. 4   10
Brazilian Wedding: Dream no. 5   12
Brazilian Wedding: Dream no. 6   13
Brazilian Wedding: Dream no. 7   14

II.
Brazilian Groom: Dream no. 1   19
Brazilian Groom: Dream no. 2   21
Brazilian Groom: Dream no. 3   22
Brazilian Groom: Dream no. 4   23
Brazilian Honeymoon West   25
Brazilian Honeymoon East   26

III.
Midwestern Wedding: Dream no. 1   29
Midwestern Wedding: Dream no. 2   30
Midwestern Wedding: Dream no. 3   31
Midwestern Wedding: Dream no. 4   32
Midwestern Wedding: Dream no. 5   33
Midwestern Wedding: Dream no. 6   34

IV.
Midwestern Groom: Dream no. 1   39
Midwestern Groom: Dream no. 2   40
Midwestern Groom: Dream no. 3   42
Midwestern Groom: Dream no. 4   43
Midwestern Groom: Dream no. 5   45

V.
Niagara Falls: Scrapbook One   49
Niagara Falls: Scrapbook Two   50
Niagara Falls: Scrapbook Three   52
Niagara Falls: Scrapbook Four   53
Niagara Falls: Scrapbook Five   55

VI.
Epilogue: Epithalamion   59

For Dom Alfredo Novak

&

In memory of Padre Adelir de Carli

PROLOGUE: ONEIROMANCE

Instinct says, *Sleep with the lights on again.*
Amen to that. You talk in your sleep.
Go ahead & run—you'll just die tired.
A bride in a field, a chatelaine who looks
like me, watches & keys on a chain around
her waist, carries a copy of the *Oneirocritica*
by Artemidorus. Next: a chorus. A stadium
radiant with kliegs. Two more figures
in the same field, like plastic cake toppers.
Eyes closed, ears stoppered to all but their
voices. They lay out my choices. One's called
Call. One's called Response.

> When I say *Marriage*
> you say *Run!*
> *Marriage! Run!*
> *Marriage! Run!*

Where do I go for something in between
& when I wake up, what will it mean?
O night, O flight, O adumbral belovéd!
You are besotted. I am lean & succinct.
Who put all this darkness in our little room?

I.

New hope may bloom,
& days may come
Of milder, calmer beam,
But there's nothing half so sweet in life
As love's young dream.

—Thomas Moore

BRAZILIAN WEDDING: DREAM NO. 1

The stars are upside down
& it's winter in August,
but avocados grow
here all year round.
     Beth & I
are lost. Our fiancés
will never find us. *But,*
I remind us, *it's okay.*
This is just a dream.
Then we forget we're dreaming.
Beth starts floating, curls streaming
behind her.

* * *

My sister's hair is hair-colored.
It is hazel hair.
The air is fire-smelling.
It is smoky air.

* * *

Beth starts swimming
above tiled roofs. I grab
one of her feet. We see
the workers burning
garbage behind the hotel,
& the fountain that made
this whole town possible:
fountain of spring,
fountain of youth.
Somebody's knocked up
that girl in the public square.
Somebody's knocked over
that boxful of pigeons.

* * *

Dogs are barking.
Barks are everywhere.
Our uncle, the Bishop, says prayers
are powerful. We say a prayer.

* * *

The Southern Cross
Xs my eyes, like I
am dead or drunk,
never waking up.
We're a constellation,
the sister-brides: one
sister leading, the other
dreaming the ride.

BRAZILIAN WEDDING: DREAM NO. 2

On the night before my wedding
I decide to become a nun, roaming

favelas in my nurse-white nunfit.
I weigh other people's babies:

babies like sacks of pudding,
babies like clouds, babies so loud

I have to wear earplugs,
alien babies curled like shrimp,

limping babies with toothless mothers.
Mothers carrying their babies in slings,

flinging their breasts out like udders
to feed them. A pregnant girl walks by

in an English T-shirt, purple on white:
Why do we learn what we learn?

Sempalavras—Without Words—
a huge photo firm comes to take

my picture to run under the headline:
American woman overcomes her ego.

When you read word of my decision,
you don't say anything, but your

nostrils flare: that sharp intake
of air you used to make while fucking.

No one is declared unfit for help.

BRAZILIAN WEDDING: DREAM NO. 3

Ambulatory sisters—
sister somnambulists—
sorority of sleep-hikers—
we are crossing a bridge.
We've crossed our uncle
& our fiancés will be cross,
but we've got a long list,
a lot of items to cross off.
We've crossed ourselves
with the sign of the cross
& we are crossing the span
to the island of Valdares.
Birds squawk aubades
with Portuguese lyrics &
cocks throw their crows
from yard to dirty yard.
Fishermen throw nets
into murky waters. Sister
sleepwalkers, we won't
wake yet. The new church
they're building looks like
a ship, or a bishop's mitre.
As the sky gets lighter,
I tell Beth, *it's beautiful.*
She says, *be careful—*
the magic hours, twilight
& dawn, are the best times
to get beaten, raped, or robbed.
As the streetlights flick off or on,
your eyes adjust poorly to changes
in motion. It has to do with
the rods & cones in your eyes.
We are still over the river.
Can it ever be crossed?
I pop the G out of *bridge*
& drop it in the bay. I say

bride aloud. G is for groom,
but R is for Rooney & R
is for room. This is not
a western. This is not
a noir. Our grooms don't
know where we are. All four
of our eyes are closed, but
I see Beth smoking, alone,
in the cone of a streetlight.
Kathy, she takes me by
the shoulder. She shakes me,
Did you listen? I'm just
the stenographer, but Beth,
the photographer, knows all
about the difference between
man's light & God's light.

BRAZILIAN WEDDING: DREAM NO. 4

Above: the filthy sky
of an unrestored painting,

a hardcore before,
as opposed to an after.

On the way to the church:
dogs copulating,

lined up three thick,
behind a mangy bitch.

So much for the dream—
the stupefaction of love.

I am the palest girl for miles,
except for Beth,

who looks like a mime.
She & I are made to wait

on the stairs of the Shrine.
The ocean starts to rise,

licking our sandals,
wicking up our hems.

Families float by in sailboats
to snap our pictures before

we go in. A horn blows
at the refinery & oily crows

coat the sky, though my waking
mind knows there's no oil

here. Waves start to crash
against the church door.

We'll be soaked, I say. But
the Bishop, our uncle

Alfredo, calls us fellas, even
though we're not boys.

Now you fellas come inside.
You'll make everyone jealous.

I am the oldest so I go first:
the tallest angel in the Christmas

pageant, flatchested &
awkward, stalking deathward,

loveward—the flecks of foam
particles of Solomon's wisdom.

BRAZILIAN WEDDING: DREAM NO. 5

The shrine church of Our Lady of Rocio is a stage.
Beth & I smile like Vegas showgirls,

like, *See our teeth? & how much we just love this?*
We are all at ease here. We are all having fun.

Every action gets a puff of smoke
from the machine. Extra panache.

The grooms arrive & we are doing a dance.

Pelvic thrusts always get the crowd going.
Someone shouts from the audience,

You brides & you grooms go together like
bread & fish, in case you choke on a bone.

One's just delicious. The other might save your life.
May you love always. May you not die alone.

BRAZILIAN WEDDING: DREAM NO. 6

Dulcet, hortatory, sesquipedalian,
our uncle, the Bishop, delivers a toast.
An epithalamion: homage to the glorious
states of our unions.
                    May you, Beth & Nick—
May you, Kathy & Martin—
                    be each other's North Stars
always & Southern Crosses.
                    One another's
bold standards & hot-weather marks.
You will long for each other like the walrus
for the full moon,
                    & if anything happens
to one, it will be like a jogger in the other's heart.
Glasses clink like the beads of a rosary.
Guests scatter the dance floor
like beads of mercury.
                    Lightning strikes
the spike driven into the palm tree
next to the Shrine, designed to draw
lightning.
            Beth & I drop our glasses,
but the guests just shake their asses
that much harder.
            By the light of the white flash,
we see aqua fish leap from the aqua sea,
quoting Aquinas in the original Latin:
            If the highest aim of a captain
were to preserve his ship, he would keep
it in port forever.
            Beth snaps a photo: me,
            thumbs-up, with them arcing
in the background—a chorus
of talking animals reciting our fates.

BRAZILIAN WEDDING: DREAM NO. 7

Socorro means help. Socorro is the chef.
Socorro wears a uniform with blue & white

checks. Socorro helps the Bispo. She calls
out the window. She calls us her girls,

Ay, que lindas! Socorro is skillful. Socorro
is wise. We want her to disguise us

in aprons & hats. The deed is done
& soon we'll have to leave. To hide brides

in the kitchen is both most obvious
& least. Why would we prepare our own

going-away feast? *Soufflé de chu chu, pudim
de maracujá:* dish after dish that can't exist

in English. Some kind of cooked beast.
We wish on a fishbone, though fish don't

have wishbones & we don't eat fish.
The kingdom, says Socorro, *is neither food*

nor drink. Socorro Socorro Socorro
Socorro! We can't stay here. We go

tomorrow. Socorro gives us bread
for the journey ahead. Magic bread?

No, just bread. *You are newlyweds now.
One day, you will be oldlyweds.* She slips us

each a medal of *São Cristóvão.* A plastic
one for me, a metal one for Beth.

Socorro says, *Hey, chin up, kiddos.* Socorro
says, *Brazil will always be your shadow.*

Our hearts irrigate this earth. We are fields
before each other, Socorro says. Then

she & the house staff start singing a song.
Clapping along. Beth & I cry, so their hands

grow blurry, like divers' hands. They are
waving hello. They are saying goodbye.

II.

As mulheres perdidas são as mais procuradas.

—Brazilian proverb

BRAZILIAN GROOM: DREAM NO. 1

The groom & his trusty sidekick the groom
kick down doors in the Hotel Camboa.

They are gambling the rooms will contain
their brides. The first door crashes aside

to reveal something old: a military dictator,
long since resigned, playing a box

of Tropicalia records, the girl from Ipanema
atop his uniformed knee. *It's the end*

of the road for me, my friends, he says, shaking, skin
flaking like ash. *But your journey's just beginning.*

Please leave me in peace. Behind door number two?
Something new: hotel workers at a union meeting,

painting signs, Portuguese on one side, English
behind: IF YOU WORKED HERE, YOU'D BE

POOR BY NOW. *We have seen your brides,* they say
in unison. *The older one with brown eyes helped*

with translation. Door number three falls
to smithereens. By rights, there should be

something borrowed inside. It's crowded with nuns.
None look up. *Is this some kind of ritual?* Sidekick

Groom asks. The fourth door splinters onto
something blue: a single wave, escaped from the sea,

quivering wetly beneath the kingsized bed, blue
like the eyes of the other groom's bride, blue

like the inside of the Virgin's cloak, blue
like the paint & blue like the sky. *I'm not joking,*

the wave swears, *when I say I haven't seen them.*
The grooms walk away as the wave waves good-

bye. *We'll never get anywhere this way,* they agree,
splitting up. The groom on his own tries one

last room. Entirely empty. The window? Open.
The curtains? Flung wide. In his mouth?

One of his bride's hairs, he's sure of it.
He pulls it out & knows she's gone from

the Camboa. Water-gas trucks play *Für Elise*
outside. He hitches a ride. There are no sidewalks.

BRAZILIAN GROOM: DREAM NO. 2

If this works, I'll name our firstborn daughter
Difusora, the groom thinks, gazing

over the plaza from the Catholic radio station,
DIFUSORA emblazoned above its wooden door.

His eyes burn with the heat of dying light
& the scents of strange flowers. Bright hearts

beat red warnings on the tower to keep
the framework safe from low-flying angels.

On a cloudless night, when the reception
is clear, they say the signal goes

all the way to the magisterial ear of God.
They say the soapstone hands of Christ

the Redeemer, far off in Rio, cup like satellites,
catch transmissions, & hurl them like missiles

to those who should hear. Insert bride here.
Clad all in black—thanks, tuxedo!—the groom

makes his sneak attack, fingers wrapped around
the steel lattice, thoughts buzzing like mosquitoes

into electromagnetic bundles, tiny evangelical
waves, feathers sticking out at strange angles

from their bodies. *I love you out there, wherever*
you are, he hears them say, & say again. His

message oscillates above the city, mingles with
a car alarm, which fades as a thief drives away.

BRAZILIAN GROOM: DREAM NO. 3

At the Zoo Lady's lair on the edge of town,
rabbits huddle in a derelict hutch. White

sequins strew the ground among round russet
droppings. A toucan scratches in a cage with

his mate. The groom sees hate in their birdy
blue eyes & white lace laced through the chicken

wire coop. Two monkeys hunker in a wooden
box, in a fiberglass tree—a birdhouse, really,

with just one room. The groom zooms in: hands
so human, eyes so luminous, until they become

as her & him, in a studio apartment in a mystery
city—expensive, shitty, coffin-sized. The groom

takes pity. Places a key in their prehensile tails.
Freed, they flee to the Zoo Lady's shack.

Man's vision is held together by monkey-skin glue,
cries the termagant Zoo Lady from her lockless

front door. Behind her, the bride—hidden
or hiding? A monkey on either side. One on

her white shoulder, braiding her locks, his own
blown back in a mane of surprise. One talks:

Your lives will be nothing like anything bad
you think you see, & places a gorilla mask

over the face of the bride. They vanish, guerrillas
in cacophonous twilight. Among thrilling trees.

BRAZILIAN GROOM DREAM NO. 4

An ugly pink stucco on the north side
of town, a one-stop beauty shop

& here—he's found her, surrounded
by women who primp, who paint,

who peel, who press her, getting her
set for her biggest day ever. His bride

lies on white paper, next to her sister,
arms pretzeled as though dead or praying.

Hairspray: precipitating. Cotton balls:
snowing. Crotch: showing for the removal

of hair. Lips of scarlet & cheeks of pink,
he'd think her a cadaver at the hands

of a mortician, except she chats with
the beautician in fractured Portuguese.

If he squints his ears, he can almost
understand. Manicurist: *This will be*

the happiest day of your life, until you have kids.
His future wife: *Well, I'm never doing that,*

so I guess this is it. The groom floats above
his tabled love. No one can see him,

like he is her out-of-body experience,
feeling what she's feeling, from the ceiling

down into her frowning face as it takes
the color of pancake makeup. His bride

will dress in fishscales, her sister in sails.
When he touches his bride, he will feel

the absent hairs attempt to have goose-
bumps. The windows in their room

will have no screens. *Is it anything at all
like getting a hard-on?* he might ask.

What do you mean? she will laugh,
killing a mosquito by flexing a muscle.

BRAZILIAN HONEYMOON WEST

Behold! cold water, panoramic anodyne.
Second-to-last of your chase dreams &
mine. Here's your sister & sidekick groom.
Here's the vista, the atavistic sweep, &
here's us creeping to the edge like sleep-
walkers. Behold! not Niagara, but the Falls
of Iguaçu: 1000 cubic meters of water per
second. O, touch my face! Tie your shoe
& regard the place I've dreamed for us.
Behold! the orchestra I've arranged
in the basin: men & women in formal-
wear wetsuits with plastic-wrapped horns
& waterproof flutes. Gallons of water
gallop over each minute. In it? Anything
you want. Strange birds? Capybaras?
Musical fish? Endangered flora?
Gamboling tapirs? Please note too,
they say you can see three centuries
from here. Behold! water wearing rocks
away & the hand-rubbed placard
bearing the legend of the map
& the legend of the falls: a god
intended to marry Naipu, who fled
in a canoe with her mortal lover.
The god sliced the river, creating
the cascade, condemning the two
to an eternal fall. Here's me adding
the legend of the legend of your lovely
wifey-face. Hear the tintinnabulation
of constant ablution, rushing tabulation
of the flash of our love, & above it
the tune the orchestra plays: "The Blue
Room." Something something trousseau,
something Robinson Crusoe? Here's
us arrayed in barrels. I will fall,
I will fall forever with & for you.

BRAZILIAN HONEYMOON EAST

Cancer is a Tropic here, not something
to die of. Or maybe that's Capricorn?
Anyway, it's dawn & we are on our
honeymoon. Freighters & oil tankers
dock in the bay but our skiff makes
its way away from all this to the honey-
soaked bliss of *Ilha do Mel:* Honey &
moons. Bees & craters. We'll be there
soon. There will be no cars, only
handcarts. There will be Bob Marley
& there will be hippies. Manioc fries &
fried bananas & a small shared plate
of *Romeu e Julieta:* jellied guava atop
a slice of white cheese. We will hike
the ancient fort & we will climb
the lighthouse. We will meet
the fisherman who fishes in a dug-
out canoe, who doesn't use ice, who
sells them right away—nice nice
fresh fresh—at the *Mercado do Peixe.*
We will evade the clamoring packs
of wild dogs, the cannon, the rising
tide. We'll glide through the mist to the
highest vista, where we will say:
I give you all this, all that's mine &
not mine & we will share it 'til we die.
For now, dolphins splash alongside
our craft bearing us safely on our
lua de mel. Black with smooshed-
in faces, they watch our backs
as our low-slung boat flings water
aside, past islands with no names,
toward the luxated sunrise & some
mountains which are mountains
& some mountains which are clouds.

III.

You're in love & I'm in trouble.

—Paul Westerberg

MIDWESTERN WEDDING: DREAM NO. 1

I promised to go quietly, but there's a gun at my back.
Your hand—clenched together to make the barrel, the trigger—

feels bigger than I remember. The muzzle—the tip of your index
finger—strips a small hole in the small of my dress. You press hard

to guide me in: City Hall. *You can't fight it,* you grin
at the sign as we pass, cueing a laugh track. The pink marble

corridor clinks with laughs: ice cubes rattling at the bottom
of a glass. All the clerks look up, not stopping their typing,

& ask, *My, isn't he dashing? So tall! So strapping!*

Step into my office, says the Justice of the Peace.
He wears a hunting cap. One of the earflaps snaps off

like ice, clatters to the floor. No one stoops to pick it up.
No one hands it back. *I won't bore you with a long ceremony.*

You cock the trigger, a crack that sickens up & down my spine.
The air thickens. *Have you the rice?* the JP asks,

& I fling it at the clerks, who have all started singing
"Pachelbel's Canon" in time with their keystrokes.

At the moment of impact, they fly up, clicking like doves.
You pick them off with your fingergun.   I run.

MIDWESTERN WEDDING: DREAM NO. 2

The bride with my face cries
when the Justice of the Peace
declares, *Man & Wife*.
The bride smears her mascara.
Now she wears raccoon eyes.
The bride is naked except for
a pinafore of lace anti-macassars
& paper doilies. The bride is white
with eyelets & she rifles in the wind.
Bright with tiny gimlet eyes,
the bride stares fixedly
into the middle distance as the JP
snaps their picture. The air:
hung with pollen. The corn:
high as an elephant's eye.
The bride telescopes to the future
with clarity: a dim, still room
where her groom drinks gimlets.
Early. Declares, *It's 5 o'clock
somewhere*. Where her groom
puts his feet up in his favorite
chair, in that still, dim room
aproned in doilies & anti-
macassars. Outside: the wind,
sweeping down the plain.

MIDWESTERN WEDDING: DREAM NO. 3

This state has one of the highest
rates of marriage in the Union.
It is three days before the birthday
of the Union of the states. Hot.
A delirious state. Lawn mowers
moan like the ghosts of generals.
Cicadas drone like the ghosts of American-
made cars. Recent rain coats everything—
trees, street signs—with the iridescent
shine of a plastic cake topper. A sign
that normally says *One Way* states
Your sister is doing the same thing
at the same time in another state.
No one's looking save the Justice
of the Peace. Still, it feels like
performance. Like we should gyrate.
Day's gray brightness flicks out
like a streetlight. Night crashes down
like a cartoon safe. Fireworks flash:
heated needles stitching lines,
connecting dots of constellations.
We spin & you dip me. Sparks fall
& collect in the Big Dipper's basin. It tips.
Sprinkles them on us. *Those loopy ones*
look like God's own sperm, the JP says.
You & I eye each other & laugh. Nervous.
Gunpowder reports quake over our shakily
recited vows, our statements of love.
The skies smile loudly on our newly
changed state. Why do people still do this?
Why go through this? Neither you nor I
can explain the state that we're in.

MIDWESTERN WEDDING: DREAM NO. 4

Here we are, dearest, in the darkling reception hall,
lined with linoleum, aswarm with veterans.

For God & Country & Bingo Every Tuesday
crawls the LED above the double doors.

By the light of the PBR sign above the bar
it's hard to tell one bride from her sister,

but I assure you, darling, I'm pretty sure I'm me.
There's the circle on the wedding program

where I've set down my glass accidentally,
& there's my sister, my shining mirror,

standing near her groom as they cut their cake.
Their knife falls through the layers. Ours

does the same through a glass darkly. The room
quakes with flashbulbs. In that strobe, you can see:

my father, the rhadamanthine Post Commander.
The bartender clad in her epicene vest.

Uniformed men with hectic complexions,
survivors of wars of various kinds, dying slowly

of lolling old age. See their fake legs? See their glass
eyes? See the powdery widows they leave behind?

The tuxedoed DJ takes a request to play Pat Benatar:
Believe me, believe me, I can't tell you why

I'm trapped by your love, I'm chained to your side.
American Legionnaires & their American wives

take to the floor & dance. In the picture, snapped
with somebody's cameraphone, you look askance,

& I look at you like you are a flare, a sign.
You are the weird light over my battlefield.

MIDWESTERN WEDDING: DREAM NO. 5

Amid cardboard coasters with the post
number stamped on, we open presents
at the American Legion. A leathery man
in a uniform cap says,
                    You two go
together like wood paneling & carriage
lights. Slaps his pal on the back, adds,
Don't they, Emory? Ain't that right?
The boxes reveal things we were not
hoping to receive:
                    towels monogrammed
with "our" initials, though you won't
change your name
                    & I won't change mine.
The same streamlined toaster three times
in a row.
              A Cuisinart iron that makes heart-
shaped waffles,
                    & four mismatched highball
glasses, premixed Old Fashioneds already
poured.
              Somebody flips on the icicle lights,
our cue to rise & head to the wall:
                              a mysterious square,
wrapped in brown paper. Inside? Honest Abe!
Illinois' finest rendering of our 16th President,
presiding benignly over our postnuptials.
Abruptly, they start to play Pin the Stovepipe
Hat on the Man Who Saved the Union.
The portrait starts bleeding.
                    We flee the proceedings.
Outside, we try to give our presents away.
Every car trails cans & streamers—gauzy,
bloodstained—but they are all of them
dreaming. None of them stop.

MIDWESTERN WEDDING: DREAM NO. 6

2 a.m., guests dispersing, Beth & I
creep to the wings of the American
Legion Hall, surveying our options
for late night snacking. There's never
much time to eat during these things.
I'm skinny as a starlet with smaller
boobs, white dress slack across
my flat white stomach. We are
very young, we are very lovely.
Stealthy, we head through back
rooms to the kitchen. Our grooms
haven't missed us & we're sure
they wouldn't mind our grabbing
a treat. Standing at the counter,
we cram our faces with leftover
cake & pages from the guestbook
Beth's smuggled in her capacious
cleavage. She eats names rapaciously
as I look on: the Serial Prep School
Expellee, the Aged Coquette, the Young
Book Lover, & Gulf War Part II Vets 1-3.
She passes me a fistful: the 21-Year-Old
Dead in a Month From Cancer,
the Indian Dancer. We split
the Gay Actor in Town From LA
& the Bi College Roommate, plus
Priestly Great-Uncles. Beth is just 22.
I am 25. Together we've become old
married ladies, though we still feel
we haven't left childhood behind.
Between slices slathered with butter
cream I describe: *in Renaissance Venice,*
adolescence lasted until you were 27.
Isn't that fine? she replies, licking
her slender fingers. *Now eat this*
next page & wash it down with champagne.

The Texan In-Laws, the Team of Croatians,
the Divorced Brother-in-Law & the Jewish
Girlfriend. The Undercover Vegan.
Little Sister Megan & her Boyfriend
Kevin. The Fleet of Nebraskans.
We're both so hungry we could go
on all night biting. Catholic Aunts
& Assorted Rednecks. White Trash
Relatives & Bluestocking Scholars.
The If I Had a Dollar For Every
Timers. They taste like paper, like love,
like fate. Fellow Grad School Rhymers,
The Cousin We're Sure Should've
Become a Nun. Haven't Seen You
Since High School & His Cute Date
What's Her Face. They can no more
escape their futures than we can ours.
We're almost full. We're almost done.
The lights flip off & on once, then twice.
The adults are trying to tell us it's time
to be quiet. Time to move on.

IV.

Love to his soul gave eyes;
he knew things are not as they seem.
The dream is his real life;
the world around him is the dream.

—Michel de Montaigne

MIDWESTERN GROOM: DREAM NO. 1

The groom speeds the highway
on the way to his wedding.
A groom feeds, stables,
& exercises equines.
Skinny rainslick horses
graze at roadside, laze
in ditches, chewing reeds
in the weedy median.
Their stalky legs peg
their unshod hooves
to their xylophone ribs.
To groom is to perform
a hygienic activity, to
clean or condition (as
a horse or dog). They
toss their tails, they flip
their manes. The groom
contemplates husbandry.
They may have names,
but no one remembers,
just like those cheerleaders:
slutty, anorexic, pretty
at one time. A groom
is the male participant
in marriage. At the muddy
shoulder, the horses
fall into staggered lines.
The cheer they say?
Ready? OKAY!
TOGETHER! TOGETHER!
YOU HAVE TO BE TOGETHER!
OR ALONE! ALONE!
YOU'LL BE ALONE FOREVER!
The dots on the road smear
& the mile markers become
green birds, flying.

MIDWESTERN GROOM: DREAM NO. 2

The groom thought it was July, but
here they come, wings thumping

in veiny drumbeats. Guests on the lawn
cluster like pool balls on baize, stare up

in amazement as the mayflies spawn.
Their gazes? Vertical. The groom's?

Crossways, horizontal toward his bride.
Mayflies descend upon her. Tatterdemalion,

she wears them like a gown. He expects her
to frown, to shout, *Get them off me!*

like when she begged him to slay bugs
in the apartment they shared, fornicating

there until this very day. Instead, she appears
to allay her own fears: *Say, did you know*

the sole function of the adult is reproduction?
Their mouths are vestigial. Their guts filled

with air. Mayflies have no need for butts!
The groom wants to shout back, but

his own mouth won't move. *Mayflies*
in cold streams feed bass & trout, he wants

to say. *That, my dear, is why fishermen*
tie flies to resemble them. Some prankster

ties flies like little winged grooms & waves
them before the bridesmaids. Some get hooked.

Some get away. The mayflies carry his bride
astray, above woods, into twilight already

effervescent with stars. The groom knows
in his heart they won't get far. The mayflies

will die, high over the trees—make the short,
R'ed drop from copse to corpse, sour in its stop,

sharp in its permanence, but the fall of his bride
will not be hard. She will make her way

back to the yard. The groom will take her
to the lake for their honeymoon, to see mayfly

bodies clog the cooling intakes of the nuclear reactor.
They will sing songs above the moonlit water.

The refrain will be plain, bugless, reassuring:
The reception was a disaster. The marriage will be better.

His bride has always adored nursery rhymes,
& last night she chanted them to fall asleep:

Birds of a feather flock together & so will pigs & swine.
Rats & mice will have their choice & so will I have mine.

The flat sweep of green outside the Legion
Hall reads like a diorama of a bygone time:

cannonballs, flagpoles, old army men, & heirloom
blooms far as the eye can see. In the skies, a murder

of inky black birds & there, his bride & her sister,
the bride, perched in the gazebo, in the birdcage,

reciting: *One for sorrow, two for mirth, three for a wedding,*
four for a birth. Now the panorama grows fleet

with birdfeet, thick with caws. *Five for silver, six for gold,*
seven for a secret never to be told. His mother-in-law,

costumed as Mother Goose, greets him beneath
birdfeeders dangling from trees: *Son-in-law,*

son-in-law, what shall you be? Good mistress,
good mistress, a diviner of crows. I'll predict long life

for my pretty new wife, & she shall have feathers
wherever she goes. Atop picnic tables checked

with red & white cloth, plasticky beaks peek
from the fruit pies. Birds' eyes show through

the doughy lattices. Augury works for magpies,
as well as for crows: *Eight for a wish, nine for a kiss,*

ten for a time of joyous bliss. When the pies open,
birds begin to sing: *Groomie-pie, you're too young*

for this, & too old. You taught us to speak in less
than a week & we can tell you all you'll ever need know.

MIDWESTERN GROOM: DREAM NO. 4

Marching past the balloon arch:
the groom & his bride, to music—

acoustic, albeit on tape: *it's not that I want you*
not to say, but if you only knew

Heels clicking over parched wood tiles,
his bride smiles whitely. She is splendidly

displayed. He dips her & Legion wives squeal
in delight. *how easy it would be to show me*

how you feel She is arrayed extremely.
"O, but dearest," he hears himself say,

"there is some overlap." Some items
are old & also borrowed. Some items

are blue & also new. *more than words*
is all you have to do to make it real

"Earrings of finest Swarovski crystal—
okay. But pearl-handled pistols—

how do they fit the scheme?" The diamond
on her hand glisters like the eye of God.

He scarcely understands. She dips him.
what would you do if my heart was torn in two

He pushes on, "Your riotous underwear,
like a Cape Cod sunset? Your grandmother's

handkerchief, blue as a glacier?" He rushes
the steps. She hushes him gently.

Her breasts seem to him lovely as mud-
daubed birds' nests. *what would you say*

if I took those words away "Those pearls
on your bodice are really your baby teeth."

Dancing, they are dancing & the song
goes on. *then you couldn't make things new*

just by saying I love you His bride grins,
locking her eyes with his, her fingers like doves.

more than words Like soft white birds
winging their way under his cummerbund.

MIDWESTERN GROOM: DREAM NO. 5

Seating at the reception is bride-groom-
bride-groom, like the lineup of a coed

softball team. The afternoon? Sidereal.
The atmosphere? Ethereal. For instance,

he's an Army man through & through,
yet the father of the brides sports

a sailor suit. *But we're landlocked,*
the groom cries. *The prairie was once*

known as the sea of grass, son. Illinois'
nickname is The Prairie State.

I thought it was the Land of Lincoln,
sir, the groom replies. *If there's one*

thing Dad hates, it's a know-it-all, his bride
whispers, eyes wide, brown as the State

Tree: the White Oak. They're the perfect
couple, except when they're not. They've

got a lot of living to do & not much
time. Rosa rugosa creeps from the pergola

to the groom's throat, to silence, to safen.
He hastens to right things. He is an active

listener. The bride's dad explains the origin
of the word "honeymoon." *In Babylonian*

times, the bride's father would provide
his son-in-law with all the mead he could

drink during the first month of marriage.
Get it? Honey, & therefore moon.

Clouds bloom like algae overhead,
& everyone awaits the groom's reply.

I will wrap your daughter up, sir, like
a book in sandpaper, so that she will destroy

everything else on the shelves. Thunder
booms like a mortar in the distance.

The moon shines down. Rain begins
to fall like honey on the plain.

V.

Take away leisure & Cupid's bow is broken.

—Ovid

NIAGARA FALLS: SCRAPBOOK ONE

Effluvia, whortleberries, & such soft light!
A lunar lambency over choppy waves

& us reeling through: slaves to the majesty
of the oldest state park. So pretty,

so perfect, so perfectly unreal. We feel
we have to find the artist's signature.

We seek it in the corner. We peel the scene—
translucent scrim—roll it up to keep it

clean & stick it in the back seat.
We will take it home. We will save it forever.

The flowers sing in purples & pinks,
& everywhere, the metallic stink of ions!

Pearls of foam, pearls of water.
I imagine the future. I will give you gifts

made of various materials. We've been
hitched for less than a year.

Pearls are the present for the thirtieth
anniversary, couples stitched by needles

of decades. You've never loved lists
the way I do, & yet you declare:

*You are the nonpareil—the girl to end
all other girls. I am your oyster.*

*I am the diver. I am the jeweler.
You are the pearl.*

NIAGARA FALLS: SCRAPBOOK TWO

Fifteen people have gone over
in a device. Fifteen in all, & always

counting, the mounting survivors,
the climbing numbers crushed.

None were honeymooners like us.
Annie Taylor in 1901—survived.

Robert Overcracker in 1995—didn't.
Legends ionize the air, bet we can't

be heroes. Dare us to try. The residue
of daredevilry lilts through the scene.

I want to tilt the falls like the screen
of an Etch A Sketch, to see if they'll shake

out, but the water just keeps falling.
Calling to each other, we follow the trail

to its xanthic end: spring-green hedges,
ragged edges. I will sail in a barrel over

the ledge. I will take you with me.
The water is cold. It gives us sangfroid.

Past intakes, wrong way signs,
& admonitions against boating we ride

the tumid rapids. With only two people
voting, we reach a quorum in no time.

George Statakis took a lucky turtle,
but died anyway (though the turtle lived).

& Charles G. Stephens was pulverized
except for his right arm, but the problem was

those guys tried it alone. Not us, though,
no way. Together forever, baby!

Screaming like a siren I slam down
next to you in the whirlpool,

at the bottom where you are
coining this epigram:

An experiment is only valid
if it can be reproduced by you.

An experience is only valid
if the opposite is true.

NIAGARA FALLS: SCRAPBOOK THREE

Here it is, honey, the Honeymoon Capitol—
Art Deco ziggurats & heart-shaped beds,

sudsy hot tubs filled with champagne & ads
campaigning: FRIED DOUGH! EGG ROLLS!

Route 104 = Main Street USA. There are two
Hard Rock Cafes, one on each side of the border.

They rock us hard. Totally marriage-core.
Margaret Fuller, American writer, came in 1843

"to woo the mighty meaning from the scene."
The scene we see means differently now.

How come all these honeymooners? I wonder aloud,
because you always have an answer for these

things. *Waterfalls = sex,* you say. *All that
thundering, that pounding, that resounding foam.*

*Also, from the middle of the country, you're not going
to make it to the beach since it's too far from home,*

but you'll still try to reach a state outside your daily life.
As your new wife, I will scale the Space Needle

for you, make it play the low-hanging sky,
first track of the soundtrack for the rest

of our lives: Leisure leads to susceptibility
to love. Pleasure leads to susceptibility

to more pleasure. The AAA guidebook calls
our Howard Johnson an architectural treasure.

We'll never fornicate together again. So it goes.
I put the key in the lock & the music crescendos.

NIAGARA FALLS: SCRAPBOOK FOUR

*There is no more simple or appropriate mode of preserving a
memento of a friend...it is a privilege to possess a very special
& personal memento of hair.*

—*Ladies Fancy Work,* 1867

Rapids slake across Bridal Veil Falls:
beautiful hair shaken down from pins.

Rake your hands through, but don't fall in.
The waiter pours from a green carafe.

Plashing water & I need to pee.
In the restroom, Amish women far

as the eye can see, while their bearded
husbands wait outside. Their bonnets?

Plain, white as foam. Their hair? As plain
as water in a glass. They never cut it,

just keep it scraped back. We are all far
from home. My own hair is brown

as whiskey in a jar. Civil War husbands
wore watch fobs made from the hair

of their wives. My hair in the mirror—
it won't stop growing, flowing

like the falls, cascading down my back.
My hair is a car crash back at the table.

You tip your glass. Ice cubes plunk
& splash the cloth. This could be

disastrous. I try to distract you.
Here are some stories that need re-

inforcing: hearty pioneers & pioneering
Victorians kept their wives & daughters

occupied with trifles: wreaths & horseshoes,
flowers, hearts, bald eagles, & butterflies

all comprised of human hair. My own
growing hair will keep us warm,

keep our fond emotions from cooling.
Pooling at our feet, it will stop us

from slipping on the risky gangways
in the Cave of the Winds. Last story—

pick my favorite & win the prize—
when no one was looking, those daughters

& wives set their fancy work aside
in favor of slightly more practical

handicrafts: hair ropes to work into
hair ladders, hair nooses, hair rafts.

NIAGARA FALLS: SCRAPBOOK FIVE

Our passports have changed, but we didn't change
them: Honeymoon Groom & Honeymoon Bride.

We use them to cross to the Canadian side. Rainbow
Bridge. The obelisk looms. The border guard's eyes

burn holes into our own. Foam flumes. *Enjoy your
time here, then head on home.* It didn't used to be

so hard to roam, but what can one say? Sleazy Canada
is classier than sleazy USA & there's a better view.

A Lion & a Unicorn cavort at the base of the great
stone phallus pricking the sky. Which one are you?

Which one am I? An engraving from Genesis unites
the two: the Token of the Covenant. We're hungry

& it's convenient, so we eat at the Secret Garden,
no secret to tour buses. Outside the glass walls,

water rushes & everything is wet & bottle-green.
Inside violets wilt in vases on tables amid fliers

advertising Flight of Angels Helium Balloon Rides.
Americana meets Canadiana. Shakes hands. Makes out.

A Kiss in the Dark costs $6.95. The place is alive
with international voices. You are talking about choices.

About what we can do next. I can't tell whether
you've called me your future or your creature.

Here, center is spelled *centre* & we spread butter
doubly labeled *beurre* on yeasty bread. We head

back again. Rigorous border controls that weren't there
before. *C'est la vie. C'est la guerre. C'est Septembre. C'est l'amour.*

VI.

Song, made in lieu of many ornaments
With which my love should duly have bene dect,
Which cutting off through hasty accidents,
Ye would not stay your dew time to expect,
But promist both to recompens,
Be unto her a goodly ornament,
& for a short time an endless moniment.

—Edmund Spenser, *Epithalamion*

EPILOGUE: EPITHALAMION

Sing it for the bride on her way to the chamber.
Set it to the tune of "How Great Thou Art."

Year of goodness, year of grace—
when love came to release me
from the burden of myself.

You'll ask a million times if I really love you
& each time I reply, the answer will be true.

Sense of wellness, sense of place—
you make your Husband Face.
I scarce can take it in.

NOTES

Brazilian Wedding: Dream no. 3: The line "This is not a western" is inspired by the Ara Vora album *This is Not a Western.*

Brazilian Honeymoon West: The gamboling tapirs are borrowed from the Weldon Kees poem "Eight Variations."

Midwestern Wedding: Dream no. 1: The idea of the fingergun is borrowed from the poet Matthew Rasmussen.

ACKNOWLEDGMENTS

Grateful acknowledgment is made to the editors of the publications in which these poems first appeared, sometimes with different titles or in different versions: *Anti-, Bellingham Review, Cadillac Cicatrix, The Cincinnati Review, Court Green, Cream City Review, Harvard Review, Kulture Vulture, LIT, Melancholia's Tremulous Dreadlocks, RealPoetik, Small Spiral Notebook,* and *Subtropics.*

Thanks are due also to Nathan Bartel, Mary Elizabeth Peters, Carrie Scanga, Jillian Weise, and the editors of *The Pinch,* as well as to the Fine Arts Work Center in Provincetown, Massachusetts, and to Patty Seyburn and the women of Switchback Books.

ABOUT KATHLEEN ROONEY

Kathleen Rooney was born in West Virginia and raised in the Midwest. She is a founding editor of Rose Metal Press, and her essays have appeared in *The Gettysburg Review, Ninth Letter, Western Humanities Review* and *Twentysomething Essays by Twentysomething Writers*. Her criticism appears regularly in *Boston Review, Harvard Review, Contemporary Poetry Review*, and *Provincetown Arts*. She works as a Senate Aide and lives in Chicago with her husband, the writer Martin Seay.

ALSO FROM SWITCHBACK BOOKS

TALK SHOWS, Mónica de la Torre (2007)

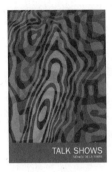

Talk Shows is accomplished translator Mónica de la Torre's first book of original poetry in English. According to Lee Ann Brown, "de la Torre's poetry deconstructs sets of beliefs about what it means to be a multi-dimensional subject and turns markers of gender and race on their so-called ears. Identity and gender politics are folded neatly into smart disses and observations on the specifics of cultural play and gaff, making this a book to be reckoned with."

ISBN-13: 978-0-9786172-0-2

OUR CLASSICAL HERITAGE: A HOMING DEVICE, Caroline Noble Whitbeck (2007)

Caroline Noble Whitbeck holds a BA in Classics (Latin) from Harvard College and an MFA from Brown University. *Our Classical Heritage: A Homing Device* is the winner of the 2006 Gatewood Prize from Switchback Books. According to judge Arielle Greenberg, "*Our Classical Heritage* is a pleasurable and witty work, pinned sharply but delicately to reality through images of cultural detritus and evocations of American childhood. The force of the voice here is redoubtable. The world as described may be a dizzying soup of existence, but Caroline Noble Whitbeck can always locate herself." *Our Classical Heritage: A Homing Device* is Caroline Noble Whitbeck's first book.

ISBN-13: 978-0-9786172-1-9

PATHOGENESIS, Peggy Munson (2008)

Put whippets in your heart and let the rabbits breed. They will. Like still-wet lagomorphs crawling over each other in innate proximity, Peggy Munson's poems confine the reader *inside a lantern, buzzing at the headlights.* Munson addresses illness, family, and the blood running through both with malleable tenacity. Noelle Kocot describes Munson's work as "free from a lot of the burden of contemporary poetry conventions, [it] exists like a small island in the fiery sun, alone, yet willing to be utterly beautiful, utterly strange, and utterly itself." *Pathogenesis* was a finalist or semifinalist for numerous prizes, including the Dorset Prize, the Carnegie-Mellon Poetry Series, the Beatrice Hawley Award, the Verse Prize, and the University of Wisconsin Pollack Prize. Munson is the author of the novel, *Origami Striptease,* a finalist for the Lambda Literary Awards.

ISBN-13: 978-0-9786172-2-6

SWITCHBACK BOOKS
CHICAGO